Abstrak Urban Consep2all Poetik

Malkiese Paythress

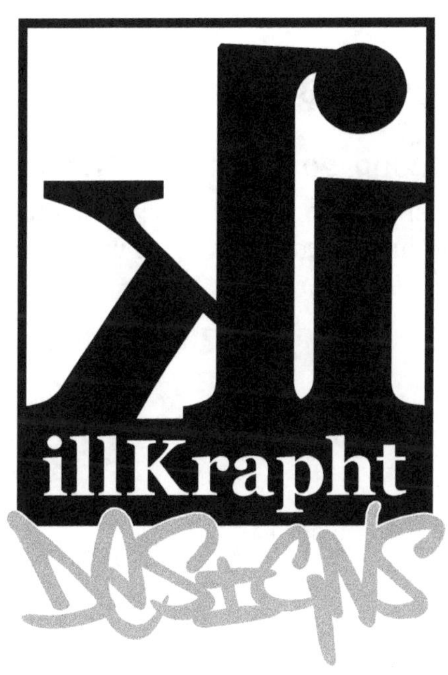

ART CREATION IS THE DOCUMENTATION OF THE SOUL'S VOICE

Abstrak Urban Consep2all Poetik
All artwork, poems, design and layout by M. Paythress
illKrapht Paythress Publishing- Cleveland, Ohio

http://www.visualcv.com/paythressillkrapht
https://www.facebook.com/m.paythress

ISBN 978-0-9916531-4-0

(...don't get served!)

Other titles from Malkiese Paythress

Will Someone Get My Damn Bond!!

Life Contemplated: Free Verse From Incarceration

This book is dedicated to my son who motivates me to write just because he happens to be growing into an avid reader. That fact alone makes me proud. It is also for my family who stood by me throughout my times of tribulation. I love you all, do right and shine!

Abstrak Urban Consep2all Poetik was written while incarcerated at Southern Ohio Correctional Facility at Lucasville, Ohio. My two previous poetry books were regarding my imprisonment and contemplation of the ordeal. These writings are more of a freeform, emotional release from the environment while still staying aware of my surroundings at the time. These poems are a little more creatively hawkish due to the agitation, and fact of placement within maximum security. Art creation is the documentation of the soul's voice. I have an aggressive soul by nature and poetry is one of the ways I am able to channel my energy calmly and discreetly while the world surrounding remains a tornado of confusion.

CONTENTS

ABSTRAK URBAN

CONSEP2ALL POETIK

ABSTRAK URBAN

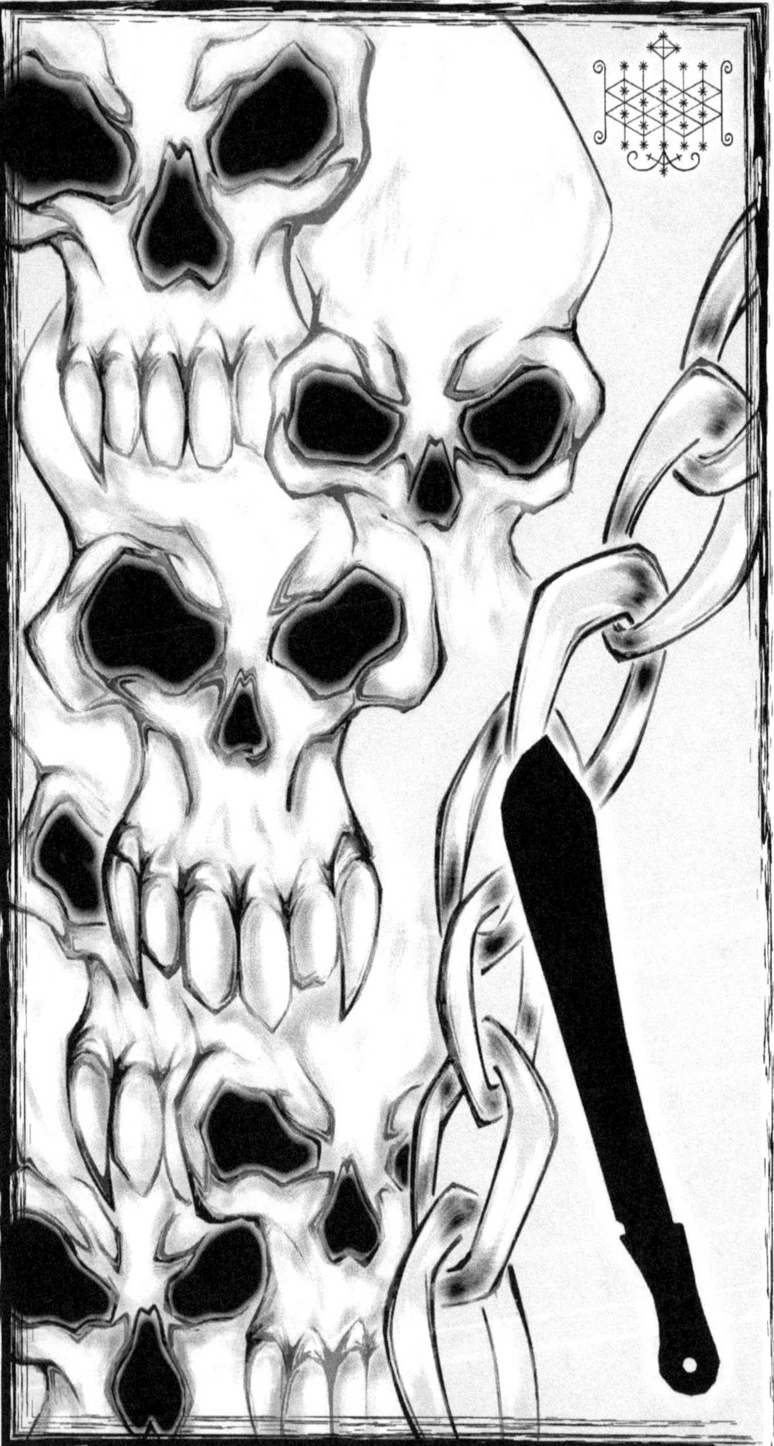

CAGED SORCERER

Caged sorcerer coming of age
ready to perform a disappearing act
course to freedom already mapped
while waiting for a turn-key
to choke or have a stroke
gaining more space away
like a true super villain
ready to break Spiderman down
and knock Superman out
then I'm chilling
there's no room for mistakes
as I summon an earthquake
to destroy all on my path to release
unchained beast
off with talking heads
I'm crushing and walking over the dead

Ahhh...
my magic potion is kicking in
and starting to show the effects
it's all my dynasty and I'm merciless
there's no slander in that quip
if anyone spoke of opposing
then off with their lips
and leave them broke at the hips
never mind the emotional trips

As I...
ravage and rip
it wasn't a myth
I'm mysticism itself
blood dipped
resistance can't handle this
get bent!!!

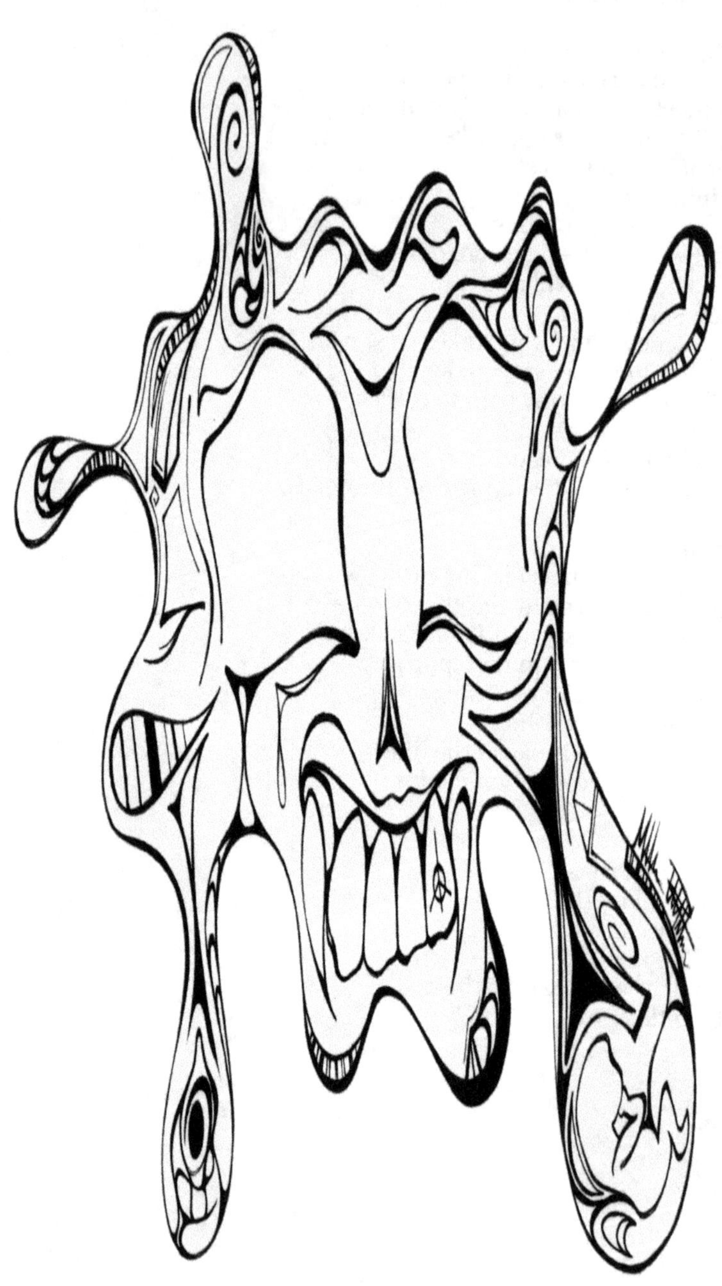

WAR SATELLITE

In orbit touring the outlook of my situation
which is whatever way comes to pass
tasting a breakdown
it's that bad
got me on blast

Spider senses telling me
to make a move fast
regard the pain last
and get into a comfort zone
so I can do my thing
slice away the negative
make sure the cut is clean

Penned and bent by frustration echoing
thru my mind
tripped and stripped of my sanity
at the same damn time
ripped and relieved of what was holding me
together so my moves now are in vengeance
forever...

Don't get it twisted
this is the voice of positive, basic solution
pickled in vinegar like a cucumber
I'm ready to feed it to you
as it is my phallic symbolism
that the world can get
keep it sweet in your orifice

If you're angered by the way I delivered that bit
Imma keep it steady coming
you'll know it's the proper place
when words start to buzzing
something you can hum along to
becuz I've been in a cocoon conceiving combustibles
for my answer back
and I've aimed them straight at you
waiting for you to make a move
at twelve o'clock noon

I'm bombing your spot
tracked by GPS
and making a smart phone movie out of it
executing, taking nothing hostage...

WELCOME BACK TO ME

My state of mind is behind the times
as I let society pass me by
so excuse my bewilderment
as I walk in tardy

Furthermore
blessings to the festivities I've missed
but now I'm within it again
except no more juice
no more gin
no more Hen'
or 151 double head hits
no longer a buzzing shot caller
so heads up 7up
that's my order hurry up
so I don't throw sobriety out the door

It's a bumpy road on the wagon
even though I know the course
and it's a chore that
I can't leave undone or un-kept
I won't hand it to the left
as I'm leaning heavily on the right path

Got the math and the science
but still sidestepping wrath
keeping my light from being eclipsed
that's a gift as much as it's a head-trip
it's the saturated fat as well as the carbohydrate
protein mix got it good
so now I can let all the ish get digested properly

Until there's nothing left to do
except smoke some black residue
as potent as hash oil in its purist
that's what's made from all of this
distilled to lyrics then I serve it
checking myself for ticks
becuz damn...
I'm in the dawg pound again...

SWINE FLU ADDRESSED

I'm not vaccine'd for swine flu
so copper keep your distance
I'm at odds
it's so true...
so my body needs resistance

I'm eating my Wheaties like my momma told me to
I can't help it if the disease is from you
it's a shame there is a new bugaboo
something worse than mace
guns and Tasers
bio warfare attacking us
along with star wars and lasers
and it's reality...

Ain't no half-stepping
even when the pork roast is finished
feeling trigger-happy
so I suppose you chose your weapon
now we need another atmosphere

It's obscene how these piggy-wiggly things be growing
and they're here on our earth patrolling
neighbors watch yourselves
those things be out there hunting
happy razorbacks be moving quick

But those Samoans be knowing
what to do with them
so I think like let's just have a luau
and cook until the beast is dead
becuz I'm from Arizona brotha
120 degrees of dry heat
will have that piglet well prepared

All is good if we're just cooking some pork rinds
ha!
and I knew H1N1 comes from hogs still alive
thought I was slipping didn't ya...
swine flu addressed

DRAGON SPIT

The pit of dragon's spit is my detox
while others get fried
burned and rocked
I'm in meditation
while smoke and flames erase the terrain
I'm gaining peace in the simplicity
while the wars carry on
disturbingly
kings search for lands to pillage
the most generous
humble beings collapse quickly
others held prisoner until satisfaction is earned
completely...
there's a maze of dealings and glass ceilings
that none can escape
not without deep bruises
or scrapes villagers waiting for one to rise
and greet the Lady of the Lake
needing to tend to her swiftly
becuz her body of water was tainted
with crack pipes
syringes and toxic waste ruined her place of dwell
the mystery of the Lake Erie Monster is still haunting her
as the whole city's population stepped aside
not bothered just wanting to watch the danger unfold
while the smoke choked the water
and the fire lit the sky
so bold...
a voice then spoke
I plan to send 30,000 more troops in
and ask for world alliance again from the UN
I never heard a speech so eloquent
coming from a soul brother
it was so smooth
until I learned the truth of the move
more death...
rest of warmth...
no more...
no charge but imprisonment
            nowhere
no you don't understand
I mean being snatched
and taken to a camp in the middle of nowhere
for terrorist association
impersonal

and the populace of the world got pissed...
ON
still I'm comfortably numb
won't be right till it's done
like they high off of Opium
rambling on
and it's still a prison break
you make words bond
so I broke English
so we can expand
it's too stuffy in here
remember not a phrase you learned little bear
I might be forced to kill you for coming too near
hush little baby and speak not a word
as the days of genocide get blurred
truthfully we're waiting for the sun god
or the rapid transit man
and we might just have to walk
like anyone's actually paying attention
like I am...
it's so cold
so back to the pit of dragon's spit
so I can see which way ya'll be headed...

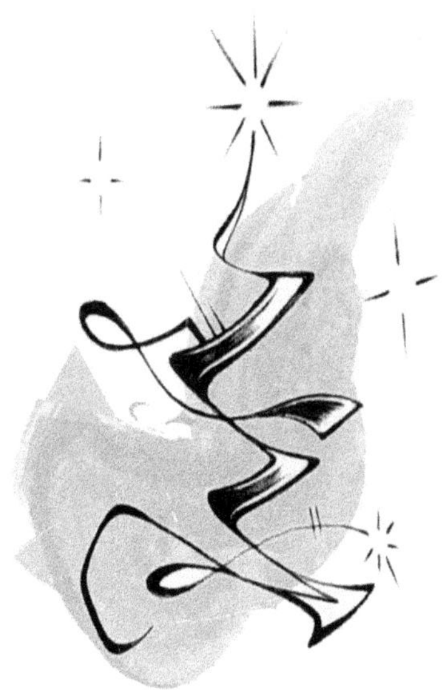

INTO THE MADNESS

Relaxing into the madness
forever young and alert
passionately
hoping the rest of the world is ready
I've organized new descript of insanity
and I'm in it, living
you can stay awestruck if you want to
or continue sinning
becuz I have no guilt from here
wasn't dumbfounded
in an alternate dimension
as a matter of fact
I put my fist through dimensional designs

Even with shackles on
I ain't worried about the climb
vibrant
vicious to meet my community's needs
regard that when stepping
some aren't allowed comfort with me
it ain't a fight every day though
and I'm not burned out
so you can know
what goes on in this deranged mind of mine
limber rhymes
exotic erotica
and serving time
I knew I'd get caught up for something
getting stripes I never wanted
making due with situation as it be
learning how to make my polish
gleam...

Start shining from within
reclusive as I am
demanding as it seems
adapt to the fire dun...
anything in my proximity is getting scorched
by arson
from the tip of my spit
sharpened edge of word gift
I guess I'm on some combustible script
another blip on the screen
traced back to ancient things
set free in the ozone when spoken

VOICES

Surrounded by voices
voices
voices
the walls aren't the only thing listening
but they should be the only thing paying attention
as the voices carry and roam
the friction is the psychological problems that go with them
there's a lot of noise following
some poking at random
it's kinda tough gliding in between
some so loud that they create an obvious smoke screen
high volume for protection
defensive methods in arguments
some clashes lasting all day
a lot of it never developing into anything
voices upon voices battling for dominance
drifting like sand in the wind
spinning like dust devils
leadership siding with the best game
the best talking fellows
the next best catch phrase
the ones delivered first class to your earhole
in respect that you're not eavesdropping though
what would you know if you never overheard
what will you do if the sounds disturb
some things aren't so singsong with rhythm
sometimes they dare you to get with them
Will altercation develop?
How explosive is the expression that caught your attention?
How much was factual and what was surmised?
as stories get changed and fitted on the fly
as they pass from ear to ear
more and more sublime

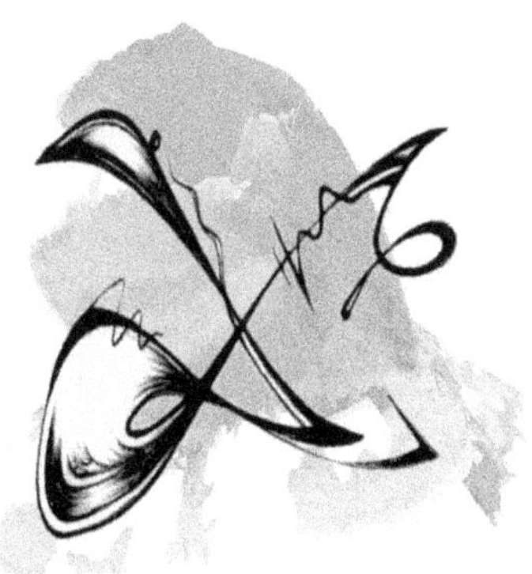

SOMEONE GOTZ TO PAY

Reclusive
            Elusive
Determined
            Introverted
Solitary soldier with a cause
Crashing thru the beast's jaws
Seen the *politics*
I'm smashing them all
Retribution and revolution
In the same cake of simplicity
Happening naturally
Teasing with explosives
at the system's proper foundations
becuz if I'm forced to play
I'm changing the rules and placement
Having cremations
Leaving abrasions as well as
Interruptions to thought control broadcasts
So I can finally feel free at first
Instead of last
What's next?
You shouldn't ask
Solutions in the tangle
Unraveled
something tangible had to change in there
I ain't got no time for your fears
A new adjustment might take years
So bring some gas to the bonfire
If you can afford it
You see what your money gets
Work out
Comrade I'm blue-collar
We might have to start stepping forget your ride
I already dived headfirst
Into the motion of the machines change
Not a tamed monkey
But a wrench in the game
Forget what your leader's been talking
They passing laws in legislation
Keeping us subordinated
Instead of equal in life as humans
For that I'm doing more than just suing
I'm taxing that
Till the government bleed
U heard it from me

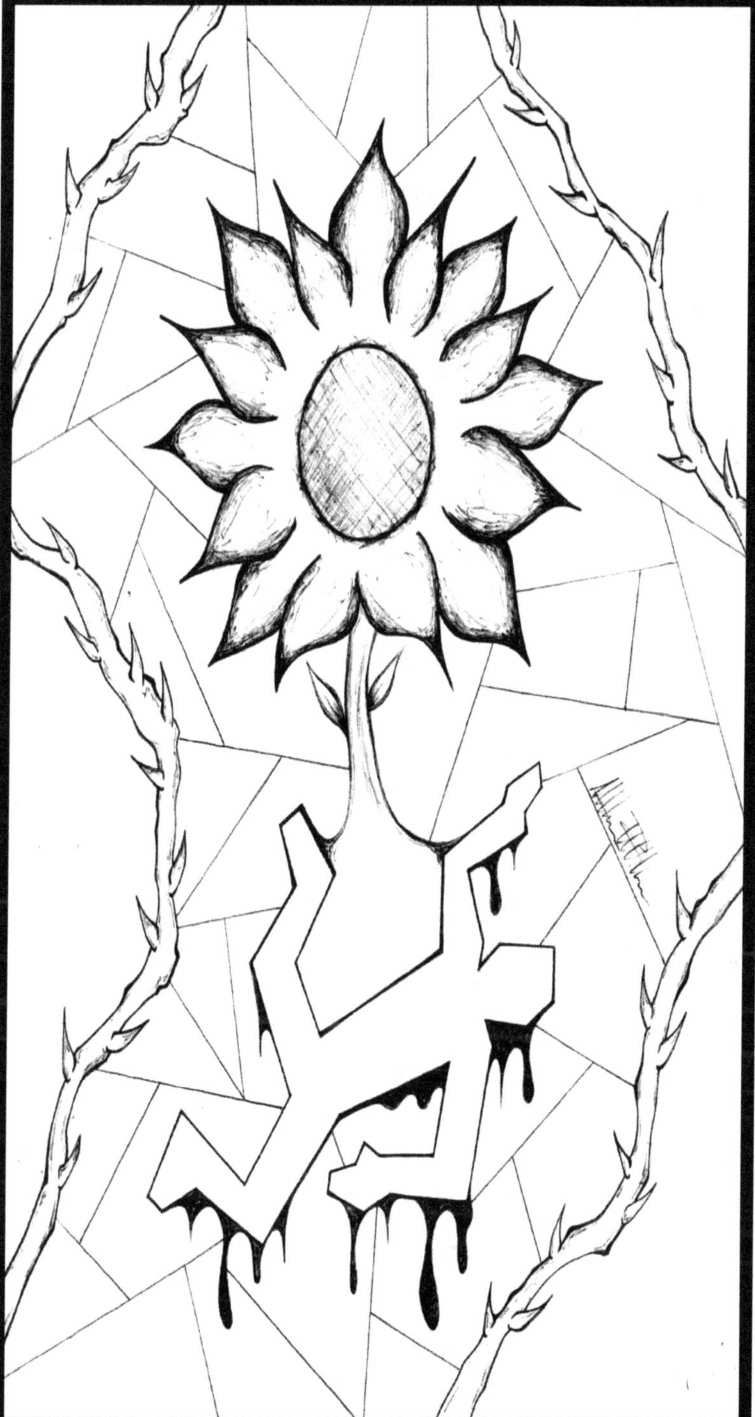

VENTILATION

Speaking and reaching
from actual existence and reality
you thought otherwise
please...
you don't know me or the streets
I let you survive
helped you out of the mud
you saw your own blood
and you're still scared to taste it
wanting to look me in the eyes
but can't fathom the depth can you
as I allow tension to fill the room
thoughts of leaving you headless
neck deep in madness
on a level you can't comprehend
foolish, grown child
this is just an intro
not the end
I exert slag in extreme
bursts of multiples
too much for your single solitary skull
so bring a close friend and get done again
I'm too eloquent to be faded
by what you're talking
you should've heeded the message
when I said notify your next of kin
and I'll say it again
while you're running down the street
to the police and courts
then going back on the block
puffed up like you own it
your cocky little attitude
can get another reality check
when I step
next time guard your last breath
I might consider dusting you
like I was the Prince of Darkness
I'm a sharpshooter...
you'll realize who's the damn statistic
when you get victimized again...
and as the same as last time...
you be asking for it...

TAKING CONTROL

Taking control of my life again
so much wasted
making moves for others
with no get back
to hell with appreciation
made too much contribution
for causes that weren't concerned
with my well being
reason seeming like I'm sure that
I'm here to work for moves
instead of making a move
and if you think that's my move
instead of a mood
you're wrong longing to be dead
red dot to your head
you can then be civil
like modest Hindu women
like I'm supposed to serve you
as if a waiter at Club Med
oh
child settle down
you've been thinking again
I can tell by the smell of your brain smoldering
smoke dun started rising
and it's not a heavy or heavenly thought transcending
this here ain't for the weak or faint minded
and I'm one individual speaking
and freeing my piece
I can't speak for everybody
How many people have you treated like such?
becuz my single cipher was enuff
you better hope that someone
doesn't hurt you by getting rough
don't sleep in the dawg pound
maybe someone should wake you up
some of us can get medieval
check it to every single letter or touch
break you down for the head rush
it's the sweet smell of perfume
to say that it's a must
skinning you and peeling off your attitude
can do...

WHATS GOING ON

Inside the monster's belly
deceived by the notion of correction
staying a step ahead of the system's solution
in the beast's nucleus
doubting and focused
prison dormitories filled to capacity
individual lives drowning in the flux
            Crushed
wanting a way out of the leviathan
not accepting the truth
of the mosaic they are all in
you can physically feel it
when the creature is laughing
and the walls tell lies
leaving some described as stir crazy
hazy
trying hard to get with that overdose of voices
got their head cracked
activities that offer some type of release
should be cherished
but they're second place
to gossip and arguing
as inner peace is abandoned
to perish
restless
nothing to do but start fighting
thoughts of establishing an empire
enchanting more and more
blowing up the inner desire of submission
until it's a reality
organic magnetically creating a fetish
to an adolescent
you see the bridge...
            jump
How many come with?
to a confined place of dwell
the unwanted gift of restraints and shackles
confined in tiny rectangles for too long
hoping the joint gets bombed
praying that God's message was for freedom
feeling forgotten
finally knowing that liberty was relinquished
at the crossing of the razor wire fence
renouncing the repercussions of past actions
working for a way to make it day for day

HER SUGARY SCENT

Sweet
sticky
yummy stuff
girl I can't get enuff
oh, how you got me with a love hangover
but I'm a soldier
so I'll survive with my sweet tooth
needing you
fiendin for another glimpse
of your beautiful moonlight silhouette
my heart is something you could've kept
but holding you selfishly
would be a treat to me
to keep it discreet
your sugary scent still clutches my mind
endlessly...
and you're as pleasing as can be
I'm sending you forget me not's
even if it seems like childish flattery
there's an art to this chore
that someone else might not be ready for
as I'm asking for the task at hand
how to attach to you and...
it's the present idea all the while
wanting you to smile
dedicated to your touch
glowing just as much when you say hello
now I know which way to go

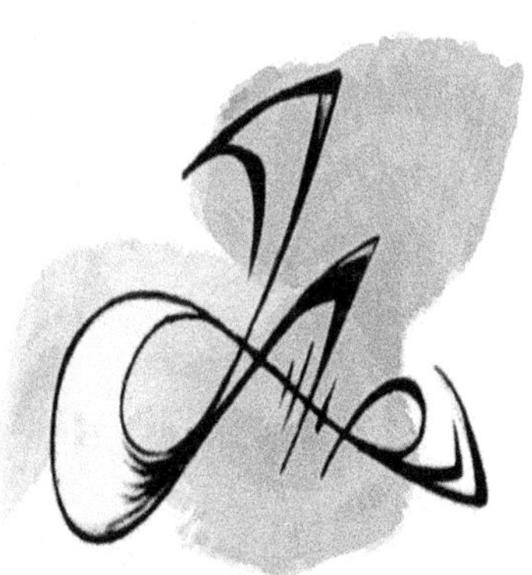

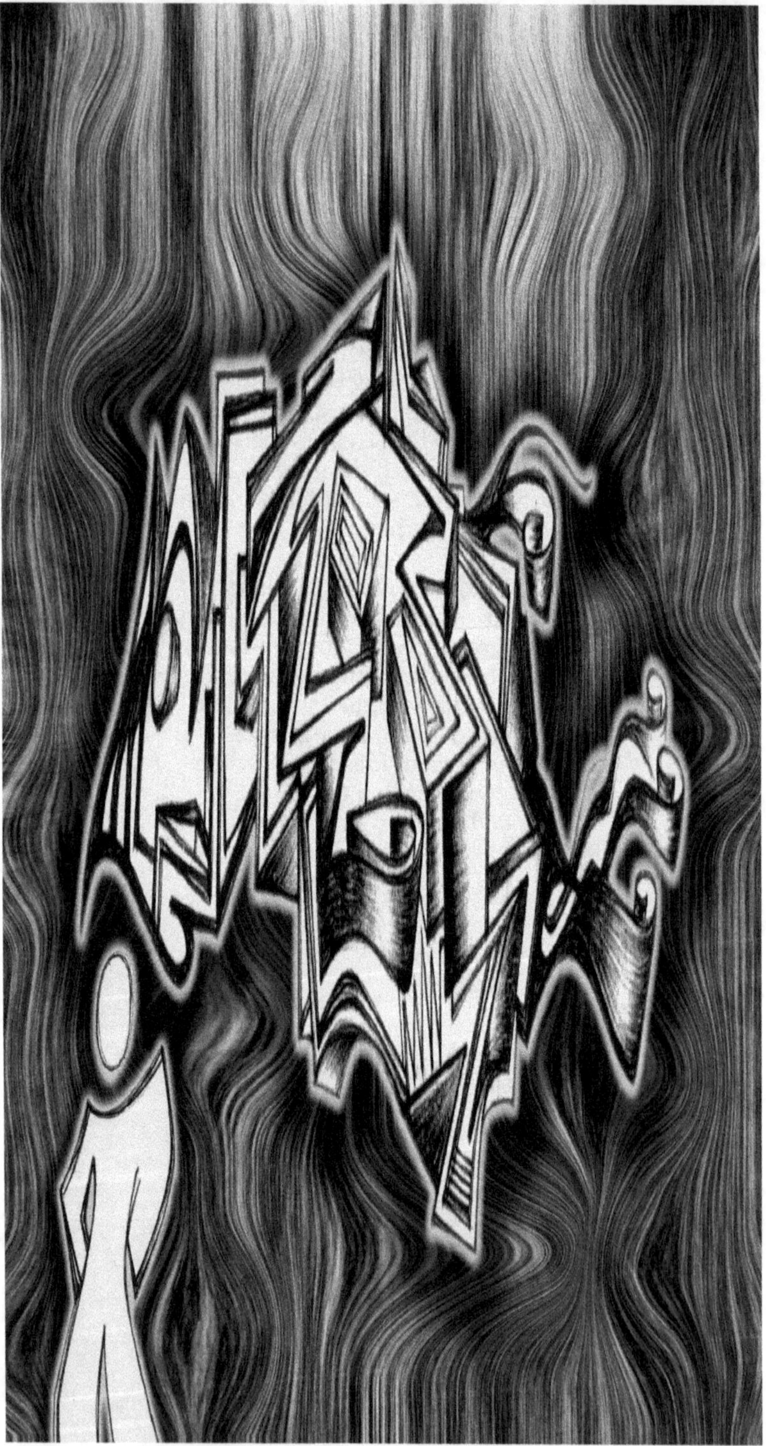

JABBER WOCKY. SWEET NOTHINGS

Quiet
Quiet please
I have a trifle
An idea to be released
I'm destroying the earth
For making associations with the thought police
Please take note of that image
As I continue on to exhibit B
There will be no negotiations from here
Henceforth
A new dynasty
Come together over me
And let the singers sing and the rhythm beat
Beat
Beat along
Passing by the long arm of the law
And away from the underappreciated reach
KEEP YOUR HANDS OUT OF MY POCKET!
Since I possess the image to be seen
I've diagnosed myself as the designated driver
For the duration of the journey
We're not there yet so don't hound me
As we pitter-patter along
Secreting the poetry in motion
Magic potion
with effects similar to the 'date rape' drug
so don't fall asleep
ALL OF YOU LADIES
PLEASE FASTEN YOURSELVES TO THE- SEAT
Excuse me
I MEANT- MEAT
Me in the right spot
Where the chalichocha's hot
Who'd of thought that
at a rest stop
we would have time for games and relaxation
streaking away from voyeurs with badges
baby don't worry about nothing
I'm my own cameraman
Hey woman!!!
If that don't pull ya
I'm bombing the earth
Again and again
And again
Until my rambling is finished...

NO MORE ANGLES

Alone
disenchanted I roam
never mind being a part of a broken society
I'm sure that it's not me wanting to connect
antisocial
introvert describes it at best
testing the limits of silence
got that down to a science
can't stand the arguments around lingering
an aura of tension
wanting to wreak havoc
if the anger can have it
I'd be fighting everyday if I let it get ahold
of the aggravated side of mental
staying elusive with the rage inside
I can tell someone
something wants to bring the wrath out for challenges
needing to try and prove dominance
aching for violence
just know that wasn't me pushing buttons
smooth operator is the calmer approach
as I slow and easily polish my articulation
so I can make better use of my communication skills
but still that won't diffuse everything
so I listen attentively
when it's relevant to my course of existence
don't need to justify anything in my situation
I know that "alone" might hurt some
we can't please all that are examining crucially
but know that they will wear out first
I'm everlasting on a road to pleasantness
even if we tangle

Society's broken...
I'm not here to fix it
no more angles

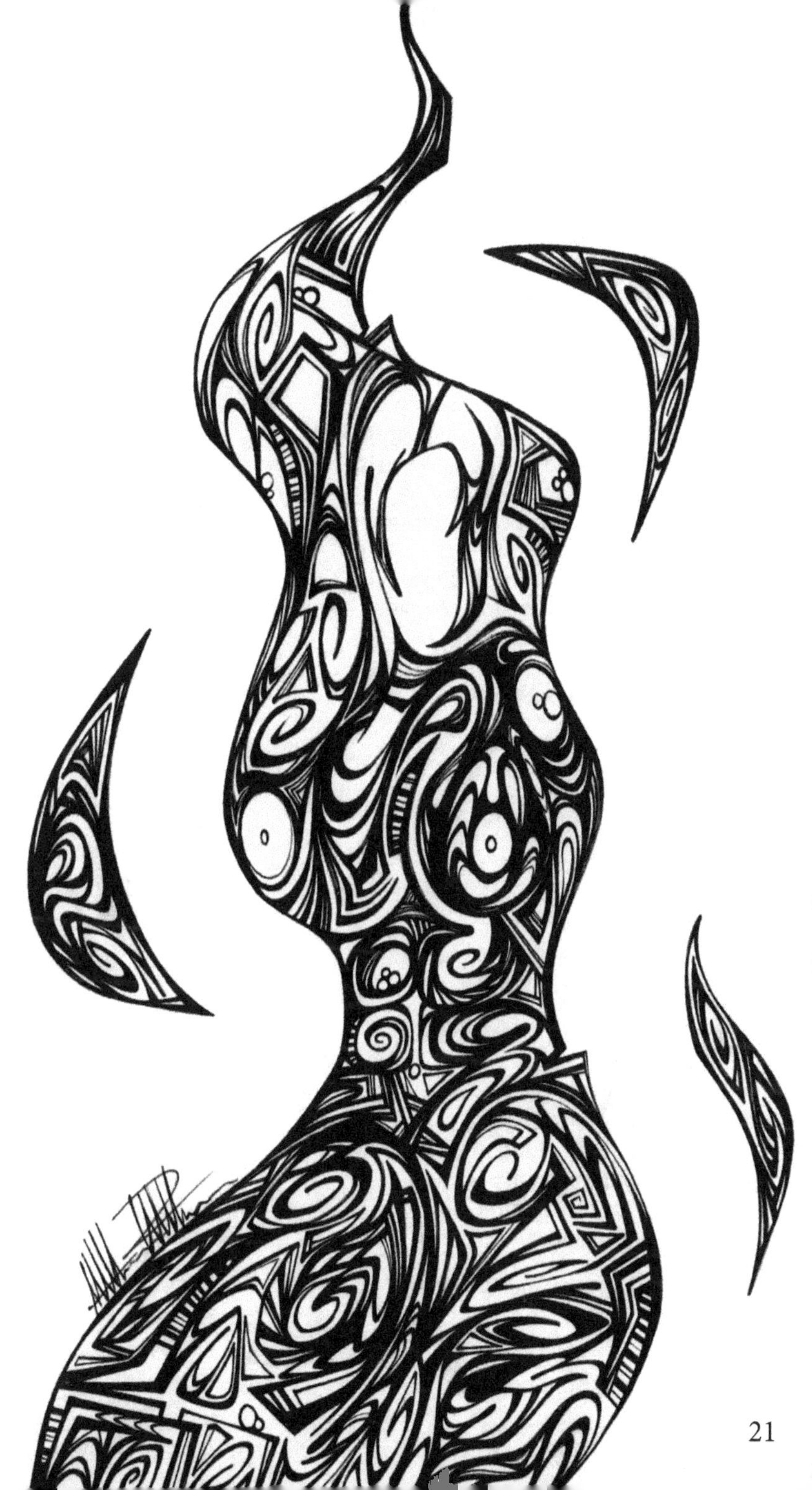

STROKING MAMA. FEEL GOOD

Mama feel good
stroking slow and sweet
me inside of you is a lovely evening
chilling you with ice and sugar cubes
tasting you it's your fragrance
got the situation swerving to that
more and more wanting your honey pap
finally got your combination cracked
Didn't I tell ya?
mama I'll make you move
sooth you
so you can come for papi like you should do
the tip of your mind is mine for the time being
so Imma nourish your sexual
and keep it deep within your mental
hidden somewhere so only I can find it
I padlocked the door after I stepped in, dove
becuz I got a little magic to show you from above
welcome you to my cloud
level 18
I'm doubling the height of nine
air is thin
sweat is wine and rain to the world underneath
believe...
close your eyes
but if you peek
I'm still gonna please
get you weak at the knees
have you like damn
he got that with ease
I have exactly what you need
my mojo be working
concerned with both your emotional
and your physical feelings
as we take a mystic journey to your ecstasy
extreme state of nirvana
making you climax again and again
intense without an alibi
your G-spot's a crescendo ride
you sing so sweet when we blend
never ending
you're vivid and unique
come again...

SOME SWEET STUFF

She wasn't a strawberry
more like a seedless cherry
sure enough some sweet stuff
wanting to treat me to some red wings
but I kept our encounters slow
so she could grow on me
before I go for broke
let her get to know who she's pursuing
what I be doing
is caressing before I'm screwing
I said her taste might have to wait
so we can enjoy the intense wave of the foreplay
don't get it twisted
I'm trying to hit everyday
get her to make a path and say
come rough and raw or gently
she worked every angle trying to give it all to me
and her butterscotch taste was silly sweet
so I came back for some more
pretty soon I'll have to get checked for cavities
or stay out of her candy store
but it became a daily thang
her love shots had me in range
she pulled me clean
and sucked it mean
What more is there to say?
she enjoyed fulfilling my erotic fantasies
super freak damn near body slammed me
when the bedroom was in reach
heavens to mergatroid
heaven have mercy
her timing was so clean
she started sharing orgasms with me
busting at the same time as my eruption
looking at her during sex
thinking like...
damn! You're having my kids
but I wrote this while locked up
so it's still...
just my imagination

ANOTHER NEW YEAR

As another year passes and loved ones pass away
the road to destination is a little bit closer in reach
yet still there's no one to step up and greet
although crossing another threshold
alone with a soul
happy New Year to time and space not owned
walking a newly paved road
searching for a home
wondering if anyone was warned of my coming
frostbitten
numb and struggling to proceed onward
feeling dumb on a new trek to another beginning
it's time to start winning
the solution on the tip of my tongue
so I'm clenching my teeth
and keeping a lockjaw grip of the answer

For that...
I'm seeming like a damager
instead of a problem solver
disaster instead of a worthy trailblazer
all that...
but just so I know
where the games are played and their angles
I suppose I'll have to seem demonic to some
to others...
an angel
that's the balance
some try to attack
for a new resolution
I think I'll absorb more before I bust back
since I have nine lives while in a dog pound
steady watching for traps
dodging mishaps
but labeled as incompetent
still accepting my hand and trumping
the cards they done played
sidestepping and shaking off the drama
of a new day

PHARAOH

A luminous masterpiece
a chosen pharaoh in a tomb
splinter cell waiting for the turnkey
to pop the latch and open the room
marinating for eons
ready to address the peons
who doubted my presence
silly children of a lesser god
there's a cherished moment
for every one of my battle scars
they tell my story in part
and I'm partial with whom I communicate

I'm a legend sanctified
respect it as such
tales and prophecies
enuff to make an average brain bust
cities I've devoured
dancing in the satisfaction of meteor showers
I reign in upper, lower
and middle earth
and it's told by my ancestors in hieroglyphs
scribes and translators still trying
to unravel my mix
story and origins
though I've told it many times before
separating facts from myths

The truth...
more wild than acid trips
an oracle with a gift
some seek me in calm meditation
others outraged
lost in the speed of higher communication
enabled with the senses enlightened
some come mystified and others rightly frightened
as goes the scrutiny of such
many becoming savage as sanity is crushed
for seeking my level
accept the enchantment and follow
I exist in this time and the hereafter
with no sorrows
as you speculate and hope
I am the force that makes the sun come out tomorrow
modern day pharaoh

ALONE AGAIN

I'm alone again
like when I came to this earth
I guess that's how I'll leave it
some people scared of durations of time
all I can have is patience
with that we can all make it
if not...
I'll just stick with me and mine
no attention to outside minds
not relevant
just confused for reaching for outside business
I ain't letting them keep any of this
solo mix fixing scripts
ready to meet my maker
the rest of the world is a disaster
chronicles of destruction
map to the math that came after is my solitude
I might just greet it with a kiss
everything else dismissed
like I purposely disrespected it
new year, new attitude
but soberly nomadic like I need to
where you heard that?
from the pound where dogs dwell
and you might hear it 'cat' called again
attitude got cold in the North Coast
I guess affected by the wind chill
but still without the boast
what's crazy
without arrogance
so I'm lonely again
like I committed a sin
it's hard to blend and mesh
but with solitude there's less mess
so I can stay clean
without cling-ons
also...
easier to blame no one
and everyone
no more known mistakes
forget all and smash the brakes
doing just what it takes
slow motion and the notion of oneness
as I singly exist
believe me it has fringe benefits

FRENZIED AT LIBERTY

Beat up and bruised
tired and abused
I fought the law and got dropped
with a one, two
nevertheless, back to my feet again
Why should I let it win?
the answer was questioned before it began
reproved and resistant I was
stranded in the deep
belly up
collecting my thoughts
so I can enter my coffin
content that I kept some of them
leaving me borderline crazy
only half the distance there
already toting more than I can bear
but sincere that I'm not really here
jailbird in flight
like a phantom
not known to many
but understood by some
confined with a cadence
rocking off of walls and eardrums
and the beat goes on
voices in my head going with
freedom on my mind
never quit
assembling those who felt it
on to a destination that's not under obligation
so we can replenish the world again
this time with liberty and its true meaning

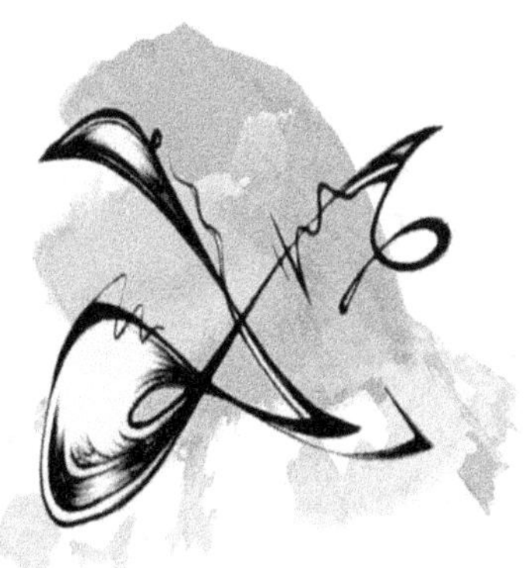

FIREBIRD

It took forty weeks to convict and ship me
it'll take another whole lifetime
to convince me that I'm guilty
another burnt lifeline
to squeeze sympathy out of me
black on black criminology degree
relieved at the thought of free
endless possibilities
and I'm making sure they stick to me
whether or not
you're anguished or angry
How's that for working out
criminal thinking errors?
outside world stay severed
becuz I ain't coming off my manhood
or pride...

I can't die so I ride
even through turmoil I rise
you thought I wasn't a rebirthing phoenix
the fumes must got you on a contact high
anyways...
my fate wasn't for any of you to decide
I'm a merciless metaphysical paragon
armed with the ability to bomb
and I give a damn less if you wild out
or stay calm...

I have a habit of leaving some in shock so bad
that they're numb
and you thought I was dumb
something wicked this way comes
you must not know which dimension I'm from
as I make celestial planes crumble
and angels run
the earth was swept aside
when I spread my wings and began to glide
the math of godbody stayed with me in stride
when I transcend in flight
from the glyph'd walls of the tombs of Akhenaten
to the prison bars of Southern Ohio Correction
as they ponder execution
I relax and breathe again
taking it all in
relax and breathe again

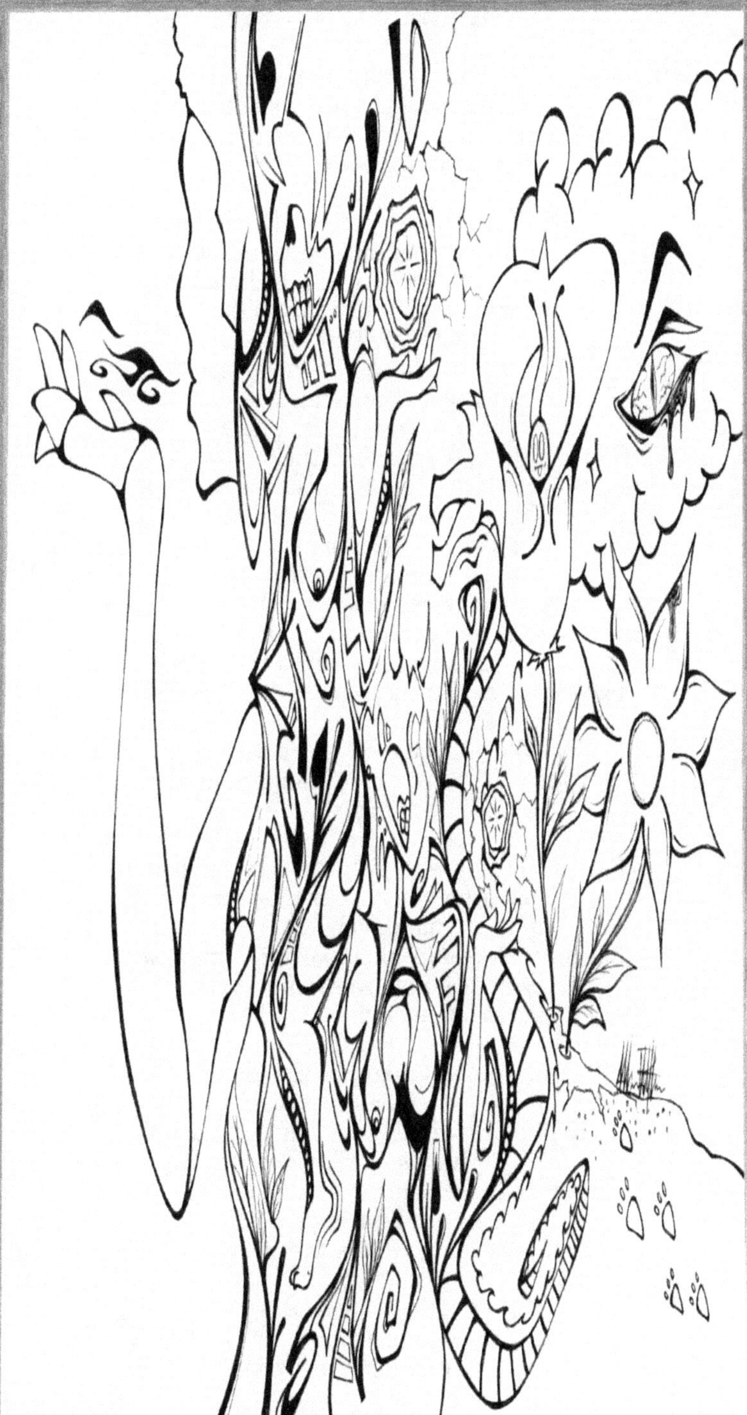

MUST BE ON SOMETHING

Low maintenance
so you thought I was a smoker
so I detached myself from lust of monetary
you assumed I was doped up

Smiling refreshed from a Coca-Cola
an eccentric brother like me says that phrase
so you look between the lines
trying to find an innuendo
listening real slow
I think I might've lost you on speed
abstract visions from here
got you swearing its L.S.D.
revelations I kick
starting to pulsate
in time with your pulse rate
adjusting the swing and pitch
to your organic metronome
while you were swearing I was stoned
so I conceptualized and spit this
to tune you to my level
baby you was getting your tail feathers ruffled
the urban chemistry innately with me
allows such a vivid experience
got you on tilt like you're having your period
thing is...

I can still freak with gift when the earth shifts
no matter where your thoughts is
handle my biz
and stay colorful in such a surreal type essence
broadcasting over radio waves
from my mental station
think I'm slipping
you yourself might be speedballing
straight-shooting
pill popping while I was painted as a fiend
you might have something in your weed
playa please refrain your formidable insight
for the final approach
whether or not you were first class or coach
aahhh...
another safe landing
descending from the rush
adrenaline is bringing

TRUE TO REAL

The aristocrats and bourgeoisie are scared of me
The aristocrats and bourgeoisie are scared of me

Defiant ex-convict
blue-collar
lower working class
with a clenched power fist
compacted energy
part of a people
looking forward to cultural revolution
knowing that the solution
and the means to achieve it started with 'we'
our awakening to secure possibilities
and the power to change nations
all within reach
knowing no sleep
already trained in the methods
of building societies
within the working caste still organizing
and networking comrades
it was always just us without justice
just sweat and blood
mixed with the mud trudged through to gain a decent grasp
of the bottom rung of the ladder to a decent life
sometimes seeming an inch or so away
from arm's length
but it ain't given that we stop scratching
and clawing for it
and it isn't forgotten
who and where inside the twisted matrix
was trying to stop the hold and control
of a destiny manifested by way of equality
and a system properly working for mass population
who needed that
along with free education to teach our children that
not forgetting about health care
for all the world's inhabitants
feeding and proper nourishment
needs are not endless
so don't dare holler about quit
life is more precious than a Hummer on rims
and your Mercedes Benz
solid unity that never ends
staying true to the real issues
not pretend...

CONSEP2ALL POETIHK

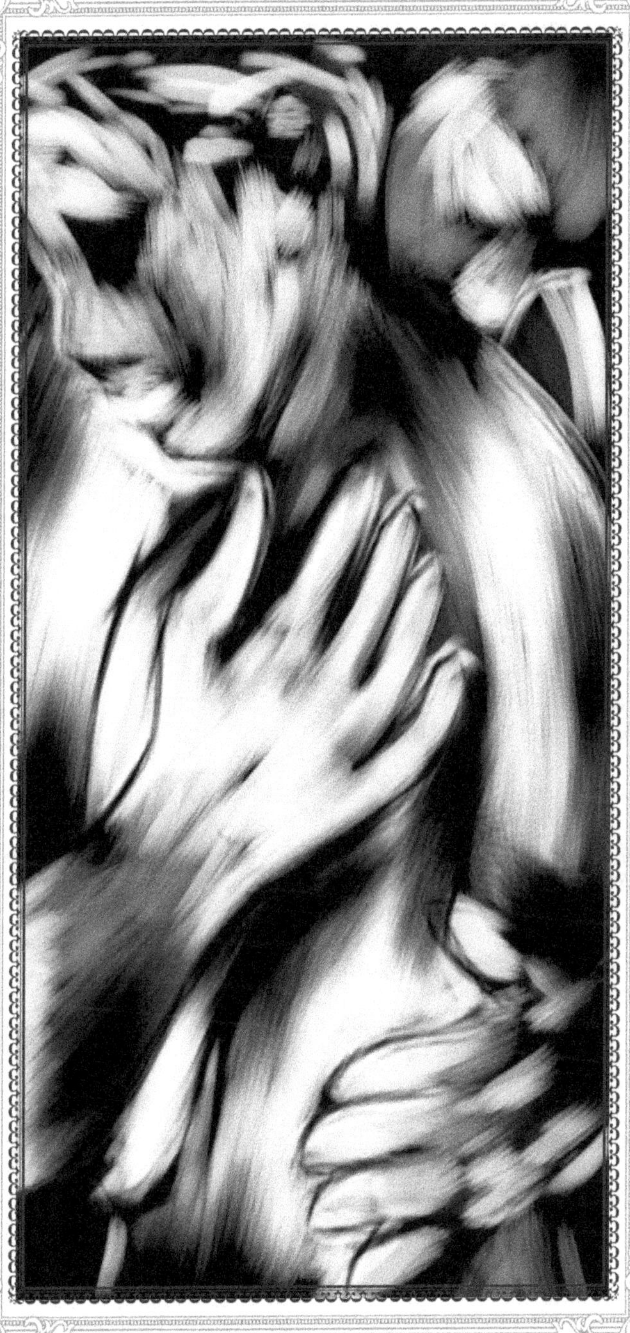

IF SEX WAS A PAINTING

With her on top
grinding so wildly
it was a fantastic
superb fantasy that became reality
coming alive and altogether
from my first thoughts of her
and my wet sweaty dreams
restless nights
and yearning for her all day
seemingly...

It was at first like...

She was something that lust made
if she ever said no
I would feel betrayed
but 'peace be still'
I wait...

Surrendering on her own in time
she knew what was coming
what she herself wanted
so she approached
so kind
sensing the principle of pleasure
or whatever...

I always thanked her for those rides
baby girl have it your way
when we would finish
the room would start to sway
the heat mixed with her sweet mist
was enuff to get me going again
I've been insatiable since I got to know her
always a new beginning
never the end
eventually putting her on overtime duty
just to screw me
oh please...

It was more than magic when we were intertwining
it was deep
            obscene
prohibited wizardry
sweetest taboo and voodoo

making a zombie out of me
like a damn fool
every chance I could get
I would be at her
again and again...

My new best friend
tending to her sexual liberation
affirming the freedom of her
as a grown woman
able to make the right choice
I definitely ain't mad
but I would tap and smack that ass like that
when we were doing our thing
if sex with her was a painting
I'd have it framed...

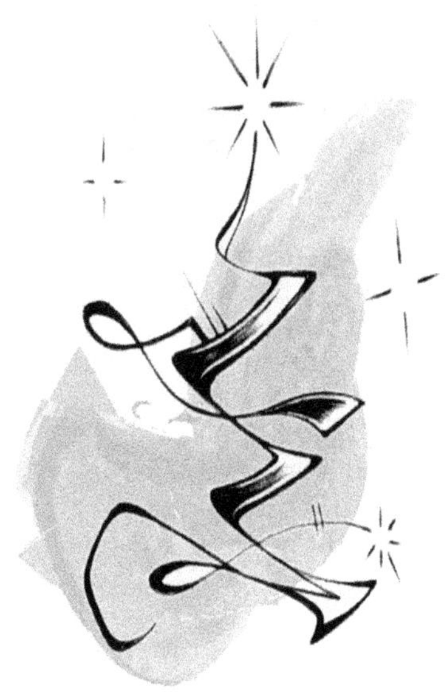

SPEAK CONQUERING BLAHZEY

Be still my bleeding soul
there ain't no hurry
just compliment me yo...
life's always had its problems
just work it out slow
patience is a virtue I need to know
moving like a snail
a foot an hour
just confident that I'll get where I need to be
see at first I needed to mesh
next came the comfort of attitude elegance
in other words...
not speaking until spoken to
charting my moves
and controlling the mood
definitely a gift of communication
even if you don't believe
aware of what's not seen
it's not for anyone to make an ass out of me
and I am a dick about it
word is bond
find an escape if you can
if that's not possible
expect me to bend metal
yes tadpoles...
like Superman I can
fly high
and before your very eyes
I can still disappear
no fear of the solitude and loneliness
as an aftereffect
accept the aspect of conquering blahzey
spilling blah
blah
blah
ha, ha, ha
all over your new carpet chambers of think
pressing out any wrinkles
in the aura of sonic autograph
that I'm leaving
I produced it so please excuse
if it's following me
the thought not as classy as I speak
-HUNH-

CAGED PHYSICAL

Prison life isn't fraud
it's the catalyst that set it off
fire burning
as the mental pays the cost
while the world believes the soul is lost
so reversed about the thresholds crossed
caged physical is all they got
hot
trying to force mercy pleas
from so called sinners
spin masters unable to trap the spirit
with manmade nets
so here come the head games and meds
they said it's for the fighting
so they try and catch the psyche
experimenting with ways to chain an astral plane
calling it rehabilitation
for hopes of a release date
all this beast that society made
and its workings are seen clearer
thru a prisoner's eyes
no matter who is despised
but fact of an existing inmate number
sometimes leaves the right answers denied
and that's the prejudge that has a gap
in the reach for equal opportunities
a lot of people say it's because of a swagger
or steez that an ex-felon is projecting
that's only part of the mix-up in trust
thoughts always wandering to the act convicting
in fear of personal security
thinking anything is a little too much
blatant mediocrity and contentment in it
having problems with population being free
opinion that nothing is justifying
and finding controversy with soul control
snatched back power to regulate
to the recipients
with the intent of overcoming statistics

PETTY PEOPLE

Overbearing
obnoxious petty people
in the position of association
not needed
wanting someone to be subservient
as the world turns
I watch their importance and relations
tumble in succession
some are left hopelessly guessing
as to why a cold shoulder greets them
along with a closed door to cordiality
as the song of anti-socialness
is sung resoundingly as a hymn
woe be to those who don't know
not a clue as to why there is no want to connect
outwardly show regard
or even converse casually
since we're not equal
we're not colleagues
assume your true standing
because it was your showing initially
of the way things had to be
pray for respect
and hope what you get is pleasing
but remember...

You crossed three important things
dignity
esteem and the right to reprove
shame on you for thinking
you could have voice with no reason to your BS
especially when it was making less than sense
and most of it was worthless
but a nice knit pick in the age of unimportant things
look at what the kitty litter brings
be a dog about it all now
but the games aren't for every season
for a time you have your pedestal
but take note of when
becuz when it all crashes down
you might be too late to stop it
looking like you're stuck on stupid
oh...
that part already came
Did you need reminded?

WHERE IT CAME FROM

An abstrak thought process brought this
remember that without consequence
and let me sift through the wreckage
but feel free to shoulder lean
mean as the morning light presents the new age
and rage battlefield tested
ready to take on concepts
well rested
bright and ready for the urban poetics I spit
and taking tips
ante up as I pass the cap for the gifts
and as it was told before
I don't need a black hat to be a villain
but I can hear your pockets jingling
baby it would be nice if the blessings come with
so watch your back
I might just have to go get them
rocking steel toes not just any work boots
enuff to make you budge when I'm trudging
kicking up mud my dirt is still mine on the solo
act like you don't know
and let the good times take you home
as I feel free to be me conquering
dough
flows and hoes
as I move through Cleveland city streets
controlling the beat while the metro police
stay mad at me
contributing to the gossiping at that
but Imma let it be
I could show you something
but you might not see a thing
so if the chance to focus comes through clean
react like you just learned about the source
of the red beam
when I see your eyes dilate
I know you comprehend me
take proper note of the dialect that set you free
all conspiracy aside
of this fantastic vocabulary ride
respond to your react
becuz you was in need

EXISTING

It's not so hard
relating to abrasions that have not healed
attitude cold like blue steel
ready for conflict
like when a hammer is cocked back
about to make a bullet explode
chalking you and what you know
easy going about dreaming
of new dealings daily
as you over analyze what just got pulverized
without me having a lingering psychosis
What I look like letting you call me psychotic?
stifling my own message
Wouldn't you rather have me more frantic?
in a frenzy about my own conscious
oh what a complicated world it is

Ohh...
when I pull what's gonna give
please I have no problem with complacency
the world was created to satisfy me
it was meant to be that I function with ease
no matter what's in proximity
Imma shave thru like a sharp shark's tooth
and make my point in turn
if you'd rather continue on in an urn
grace be unto your cremation
see I still keep my table manners clean
as the dust wastes away in jealousy
blown away in the eternal winds of change
as I'm refreshed in life by lightning strikes
charting my own domain
knowing no songs of shame
never upstaged in the scenes I made
you think effervescence left
but you're wrong
it stayed
I own the gift it gives
you might wish me dead but still I live
existing
completely
sinisterly

SIDESTEPPED DISASTER

Explosive!!!
so much for calm situations
combative
to hell with consultations
violent with a history
still meant to trump over misery
last man standing
without a guilty plea
try and find me riding dirty
I'm over thirty
without a kootie-bop
grown man
no following
knowing where and when the drama stops
ending up on top
making all the rest drop
when events start to pop
pop
pop
duck if you feel the need
divided we fall
not me
alive and surviving without having a seat
you swear it was something I've seen
How sweet could it all be?
judged by twelve
never enough and always too many
imagine the hypocrisy
as crazy as it seems
live and let die
life profile
got 'em witnessing for the prosecution
all bridges stay burnt
Who else is testifying?
---Pause---
for a second so I can strike another match
another connection gotta close
so we don't get too attached
baby it bee's like that sometimes
make my move before you drop a dime
there's a life facing temptation
and it's mine
all the time thinking I'm too kind
and half your world thought like
I ain't have pride

take another step away
from the fire in my eyes
praying for my downfall
so disappear before I rise
just know that I sidestepped disaster
so I could leave the haters deprived

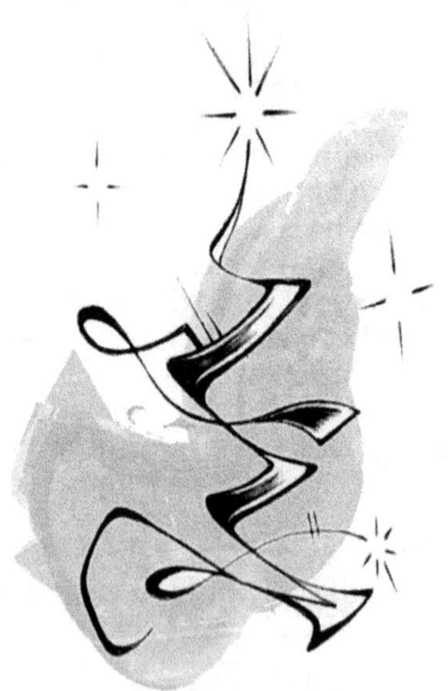

STRONGER THAN JUST WORDS

Explicitly delicious
the girl was lusciously exotic
a little older
the vet must've mastered the art of sex
kicking it to me with her beautiful accent
entering her realm by choice
I lost my free will when I stepped in
still wondering if I was ready
for mature sexual craving and affection
uncontrollable lust isn't always a bad thing
she said I was so humble
teasing me with her kiss
you know what that eventually brings
something I didn't want to miss
my thoughts flashing triple X
trying not to diss
becuz I'm loving her so bad
there's nothing she could do to make me mad
nirvana achieved when she connected with my chi
rocking steadily
her body
liquid to touch
vibing so much
that I had to trust her intuition
she unlocked and popped my ignition
thank god she wasn't playing me like a simpleton
I'm still somewhat a simple man
and she could read it in my eyes
she had an answer for my what
when
who and why
today with her is a good day
every time she comes around
I'm hoping she stays
her foundation work is strong
she ain't about to break
combining with her bliss
bless heaven for how she was made
and the power to persuade
it was hers
but try to understand
it's stronger than just words

THOUGHTS GLIDE

Synchronized to the slow rotation of the earth's spin
laying a day's work to rest
so I can wake up and do it again
thoughts gliding in my free mind
imagination focused galaxy wide
visions occupying my time
aiming nosebleed high
disagree or accept it
incorporate and respect it
I'm walking that path
becuz I built it
while ya'll was hollering about represent
what's faithful remains true
What's more for a man to prove?
everybody begging for proof
and don't know what to do
loc-up before my shine starts to blind
I'm from the sun that I walked thru
comfortably brand-new
damn outside views
someday things will change
I heard you saying in your prayers
so I flipped and switched gears
about the destination
I'll let you know when we're there
reflect light given
You still living?
that's God's mercy with direction
now start absorbing
I ain't just talking
I'd rather call it stimulating the motion
you might be forcing a fix
needing attachment
grabbing at it
wondering what an addiction is
please
no need for me to slide you this
you walking dead into it freely
words ain't the swerve
it was your think and how things could be
giving you a pathway with brain play
riding alpha and theta waves to a New Jerus
just like your soul knew

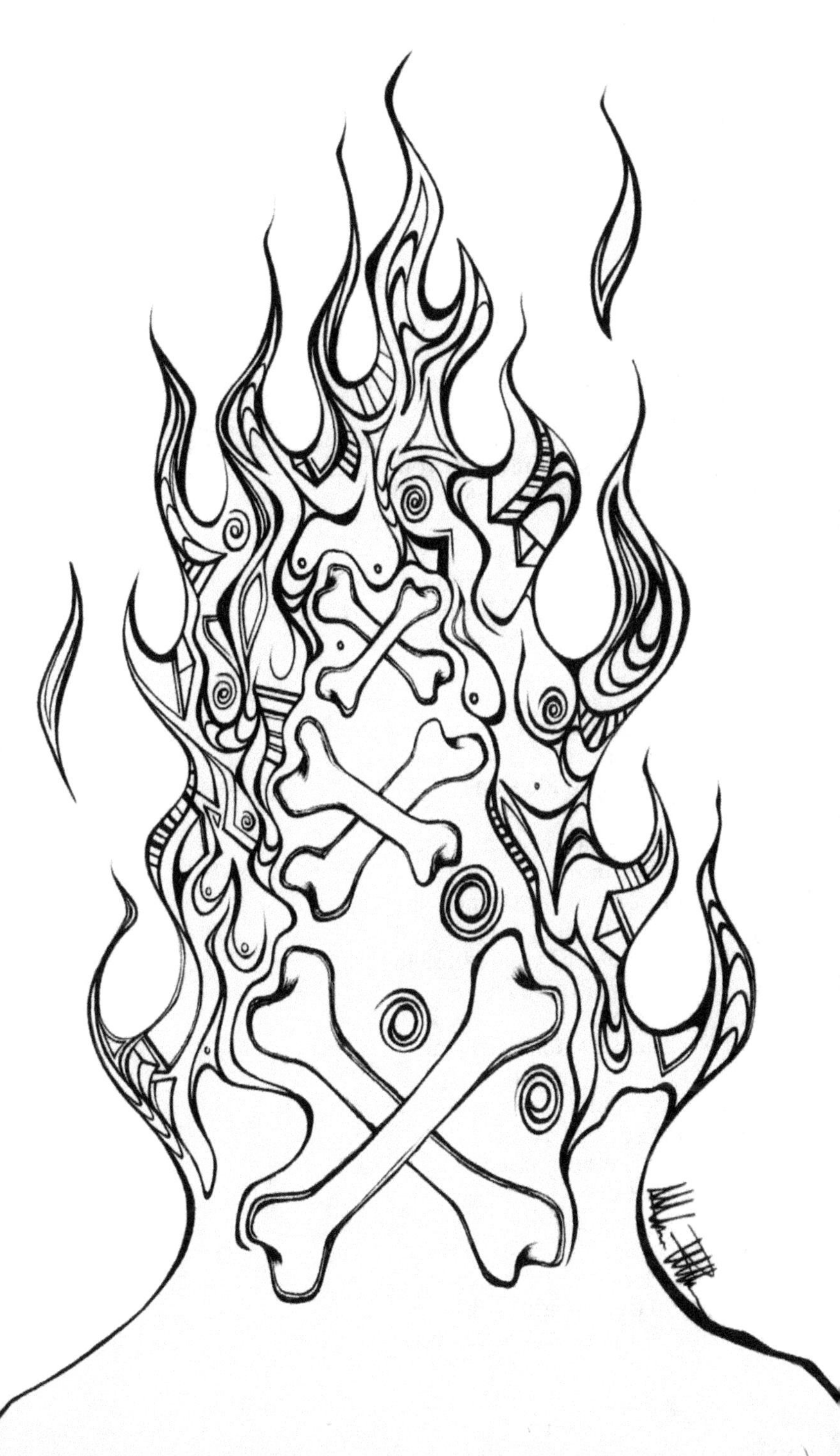

HER SEX TRUTHS

I don't need your fidelity
I just want your sex baby
the feel of your front and rear bumpers
constantly pressing against me
loving me for extended periods of time
let's just bump and grind
you know how right I am
soothing you with a slow jam
let's go play with the webcam
and have a moment to remember
you've got a hidden fetish for your best friend
go get her
I got plans to make your lust sizzle
playing with what's tempting in your skull
creeping towards your hotspot
little by little
what I'm getting at ain't dull
I'm just comfortably working pull
becuz you need some enchantment in your life
so don't blame me if you close your eyes
and get hypnotized
lovely lady
lay you down on the floor
for a magic carpet ride
rock you on every single side
of your body and mind
unlocking the paradox of paradise
on an earthly plane
paying attention to your G-spot
playing with it nonstop
drive you insane until you're tamed
just to get your wild side free
and catch it again
glory be to the dark desire in you
I won't play you for a fool
just freak and make you ooze
open to your sex truths
and I admit I brought tools
that I know I'll use
kicking it to you candidly
cuz you're candy
and I'm due for a treat
I got my grip damn tight
and we might becuz you're sticky...

DAMN NEAR BLOODTHIRSTY

I see her in the fire of my fantasies
occasionally catch a glimpse of her
in my restless dreams
thoughts of her are comforting
but I know she is everlasting darkness
and it isn't scaring me
I'm damn near bloodthirsty myself
fangs be tingling
she's got a scent and taste I need
just do me right baby
becuz if I'm hungry like a wolf
Imma come hunting
for my said desires
leaving me in limbo with lust
could make me too tired for anything else
but wouldn't she love that game

Ha-ha
at least it would leave me in her range and reach
I'm not desperate neither is she
but she's about to get besieged
her body be calling for me
and I'm not so sure she's ready still...
she should know about the games she be playing
a grown woman with a wild side
should know who she's attracting

Girl...
don't get confused now
been in my sights ever since I heard you growl
pleased to meet you it wasn't too soon
that my senses picked up the give
of that womanly essence
as we pull up parallel
let's go ahead and represent
becuz we're the baddest in this jungle
and queen you make it evident
addressing you finally in first person
so I can undress you right before me
get you a little wet
so you can soak shimmering
loving you still standing
finally have a seat and let's close the doors
for the next
so we can make this triple X

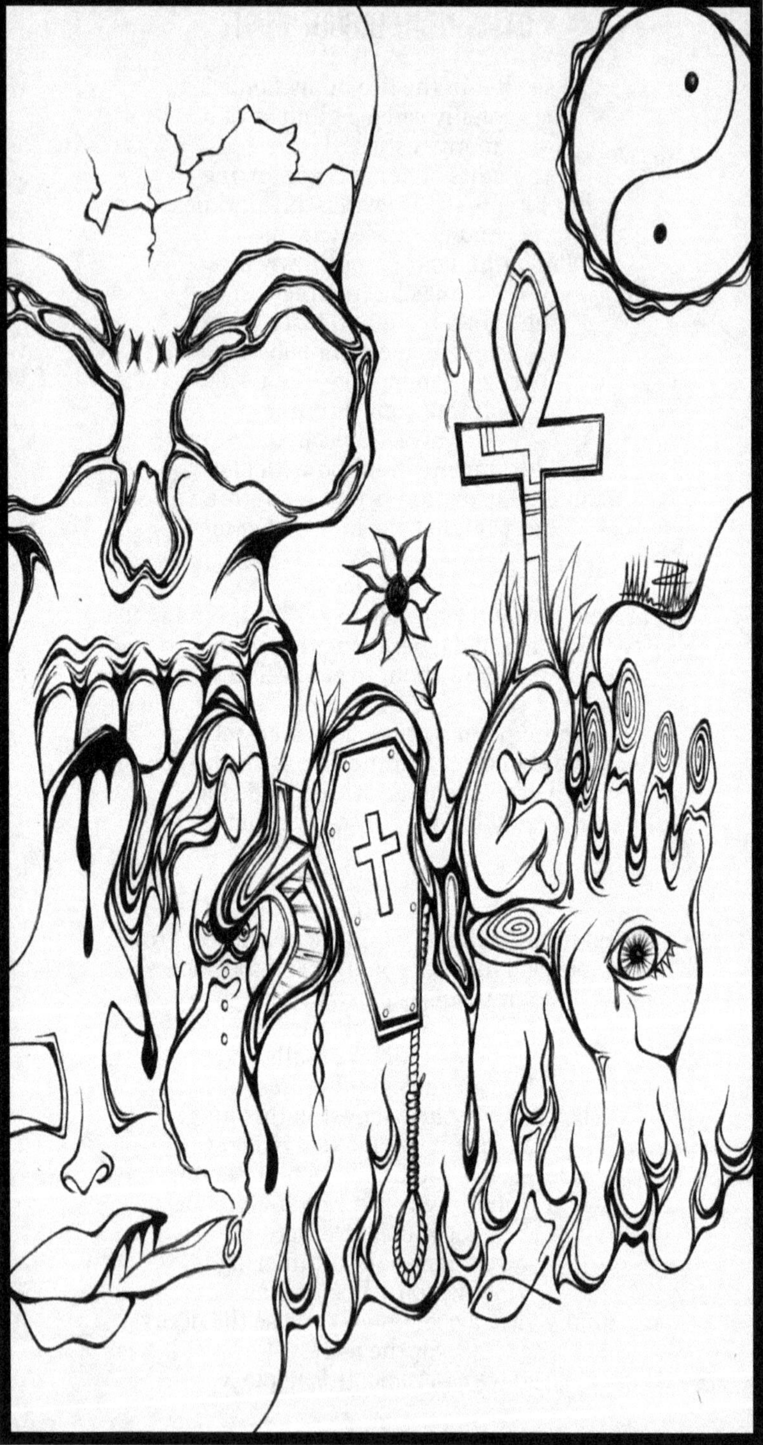

SENTENCED TO DEATH

The whole earth was given to my sword
I let it live though becuz I was bored
I then let it stray
so it could taste freedom
just a little bit more
so as I again tighten the reigns
don't whine and cry 'what for'
I've shown my turn of mercy
What more?!
so I can again be the villain by choice
like I care if your eyes get moist
your best bet is to prepare for peace to be destroyed
an end to all petty joy
it's been a nuisance since it came to bloom
a change can't be too soon
I'm moving the whole planet to the side
to make room
there's more important matters to tend to
foolishness is that wish wanting to save it
intergalactic disaster is your new master
learn to pray to it
as I begin to offer slain sacrifice
rebirthing ancient passage rights
as vicious as they get
having no pity with this divine message
while you're hoping for an act of deliverance
and redemption
I hold no second-guessing for what's been transmitted
concerning the ultimate action
you thought it was sweet
you got it bad son
Thought it was all good?
A chance?
this planet doesn't have one
nowhere to escape to
nowhere to run
victimized by an external immortal
state of being
too much benevolence was shown already
the burden of its existence is too heavy
as one more planet dies
another whole star was made ready for birth
and as your uncertain life fades
until it's gone
god bless the new as kingdom comes...

RAINCLOUD

Gone for so long that
my mind has become an emotional ammo dump
so much input
an angry criminal menace is what people think
I'm unconcerned about being unleashed
but a little reserved about attitudes when released
the world I know
isn't waiting for a convict to catch up
might even be disgusted
so it's best to remember the love
right now
because the streets are waiting
to trip a man with bad luck
another one bites the dust
and tastes the sand kicked in the face
it's not easy to step away from the block mentality
but it might be a race
quickening of the spirit
who's the first to disassociate from malice?
that might be all you get
so keep freedom as a matter of mention
always
without all the head games
and try not to get played
there's a way out the mess
child take the right steps
that movement might save your life one day
or another
this
that
or when you first feared the stranger in passing
critiquing the dark stroll
yet
not knowing a thing about his soul

That's just me with my raincloud overhead

LIVING UNFORGIVEN

Walk away
silent as the shadows
there's not so much to say
as night belongs to the day for now
the cage is the state offering stay
the blockade another man made
the obstacle to escape
if only there could be another way
razor wire checking the mood
daring you to move
but what's there to go home to
every bridge burned
nothing new learned
and melancholy is the only true friend
nothing else too certain
as life gets spent
everything clouded by regret
without sympathy
without the chance to change events
leading to your present situation
trapped and living unforgiven

PUBLIC SERVICE ANNOUNCEMENT

Dimensions open like a broken window
look and remember what was seen
as focus levels out
understand what it means
we are all creatures
unique
in the bigger picture
visitors in space
traveling at various speeds
so hitchhike if you have to
and be sure to get there on time
without dropping dimes

OUR FANTASY WORLD

Trapped in an unwanted fantasy
exposed to big brother watching
more than closely
country's population
becoming underpaid video stars
in video wars
eyes glued to crime shows on boob tubes
wake up...

Who's the wizard behind the scene hiding?

Got people crying and losing everything
while being watched on television screens
walk the block and be spotted
by cameras checking for your personal whereabouts
something stranger than science fiction
mechanical eyes and computers
cross referencing your vehicle's plates
and driver's license
right outside your homes
you are not alone
so beware of the gestapo

Who are you submitting to?

Choose...
sex...
violence...
or is it that a police state
has got you paranoid and hyper-tensed
hey comrade...

Where are you gonna hide today?

It's all fair in the games the government plays
so don't cry foul if they peeped you from a cell phone
citizens on patrol
GPS tracking you
got a hole in your private dynasty
a mole reporting and monitoring
movements and places of being
all part of a new world order
that's centuries in the making
strategically put together to shape things
for positioned kings...

FOR THE HEADRUSH

Conceited
absolute
and partially insane
still confident for a move in the right place
and deranged
so many ways to describe
but only one way to fly
furthermore
the ledge knows what's coming
good game hunting for a play
most regards for casualties in the way
but no more listening to what they say
searching for sympathy
slowing the day
another victory is only a moment away
destroying everything unpleasing
like the once great city of Pompeii
pompous spectators
pondering the poise demonstrated
leaving with irregular heartbeats
any opposition must've been sleep
the legend eligible to examine the whole
is still reclusive as can be
not quite for the naked eye to see
you'd be staring into an eclipse of light
trying to lock optics
with a being so serious
paying much attention to your pulse
tic tic
ticking
following the scent of blood
pumping in your veins
engulfing you in the essence of everlasting energy
that remains overtaking the sentiments
once held for personal gratification

Come along as part of the brood now
as you accept the change of mood
getting you white hot so you can overcome the blues
say what you choose
but remember the mercy shown
before opinion sets in
not withstanding
the survival of your experience
no matter its circumference

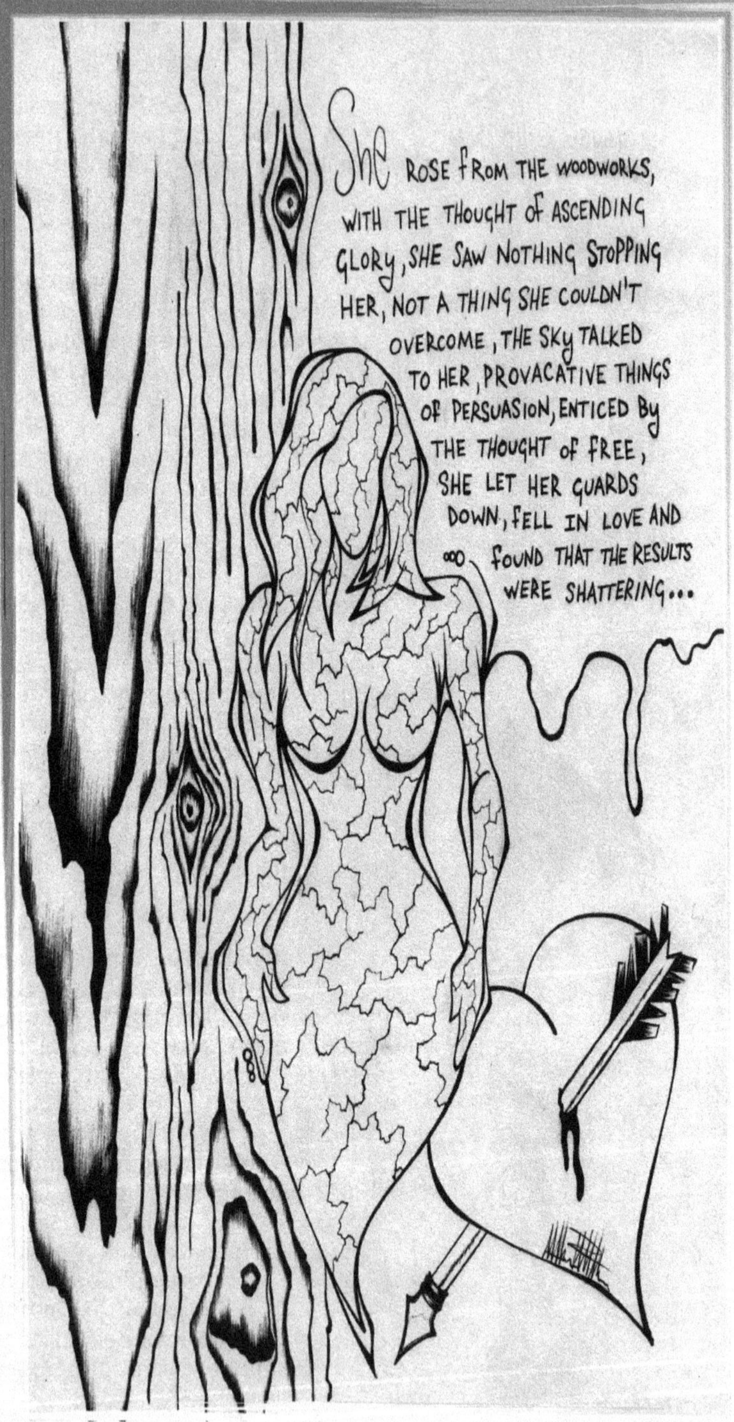
She rose from the woodworks,
with the thought of ascending
glory, she saw nothing stopping
her, not a thing she couldn't
overcome, the sky talked
to her, provacative things
of persuasion, enticed by
the thought of free,
she let her guards
down, fell in love and
found that the results
were shattering...

CHAOS STAYED

Hours piled up for corrective purposes
psyche medication to aid rehabilitation
with multiple techniques to subdue and restrain
What's the worth of all this?
to make a wild man tame
What if the doctors and officers misread the whole thing?
condemning men and women
and making them insane
psychologically traumatized
because of too many head games
as society slowly fades away
in the chaos that stayed

SWING LOW

Enuff angel warfare to last for years
and God saw it in a single day
bombs away
Who's to say that you'll make it?
while another living being had to pay
remembering that we're all faulty
salty and waiting for an aid
sweet chariot swinging low
is slow in its coming
hope your legs are strong
we might have to start walking

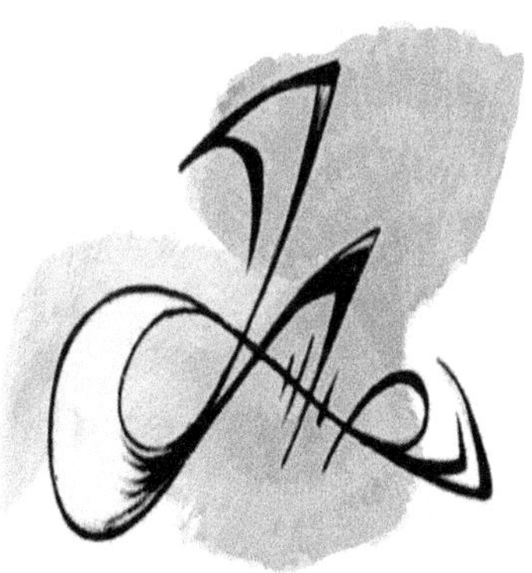

LAID TO REST

No more petty drama
without you
oh captor
enuff of your mental torture
had to force you to cease and desist
not wanting to bring others into the mess
that was made of overblown situations
walk away and be blessed
arguing leaves too much wasted
hopefully you can learn from departure
and silent solitude
becuz people aren't to bicker with you
and everything you project
without respect for the inhabitants surrounding
your space is too quarrelsome
what's crazy is that anyone who gets too close
is played for dumb
it's an instant lesson for your character
What can come from a disaster?
don't need to show it
others aren't ready and wanting
just keep the mishap to yourself
I know it's burning like a fresh welt
that's all that needs to be addressed
and laid to rest
for the final show
RIP can be a good thing
Whatever that means?
becuz you ain't said nothing but a word
however absurd
not something to dwell on or use
to make bonds
stay detached
you're better off
and pay the cost
again and again
until you work out wrath and rage
believe it
we're all doing the same

ARISTOCRATS GET AWAY

Just another execution when a citizen dies
that's how the system views it
but you'd be a cold-blooded man to say it
without humane concern for casualties
as our leaders continue bloodshed casually
money motions
toxic potions
and imperialistic notions
damning the working caste
from the seclusion of private golf courses
and multileveled mansions
all the while subjecting armless
legless children to war machines
but it's seen as a costly sin
to let the same children eat
possible food money being spent on bullets
fighter planes and gasoline
shelter possibilities
turned into exclusive shopping plazas
instead of housing
even though an X-amount of population
is struggling with poverty
How many times do we have to translate?
and relay the message that our people are starving
while congressmen and senators
are spending taxpayer money
on Gucci and Armani
worldwide comrades and brethren
are trying to survive on a dollar
if blessed two
stretching that day to day
resources set aside for correction
and rehabilitation
still not producing the means
for quality inmate education
capitalist modern slavery
snatching up more and more of the poor
giving them to the prison beast
society brainwashed into submission
by torturing war regimes
and the aristocrats get away Scott-free

MATING GAMES

Reading your sensual body motion
sexy notions
my eyes taking in everything
slowly as we progress
onward to a comfortable state of relaxation
for both of us
continuing on with a little bit of lust
warm with a private evening
of passionate affection and trust
tickling you with tingles every time we touch
slow me down if it seems like we've rushed
love you much
eat you for lunch
dinner and breakfast
keep you on a wonderland carpet ride
ecstatically high
as I'm playing in your pudding pie
kitty cat
I'm at yours just like that
ease into a magic world
I'm your escort and curator
disciple and conductor
still open for interpretation
so you don't catch claustrophobia
if it seems bright
that's the shine of classic polish
you deserve that piece of knowledge
I'll make it rain
if that's what your souls calling for
adjusting to fit you sexually
caramel candy
floating indeed
get you giggling like a telewubby
girl you're going the scenic route with me
knowing I got what you need
that's my creed and credentials
marinate a little while
you know
when all signs say go
remember
I'm patient in waiting until then
homie-lover-friend
ladylove you know what time it was
when our eyes first connected
and the physical feeling complemented

I got so many reasons why
that you'd be tripping and you're still a godsend
if I have a hard time keeping you
I'll make the laws of reality bend
leaving it for the mystics to explain
anyways
just know that Cupid aimed
as all is fair when we play those mating games
I'm glad you came

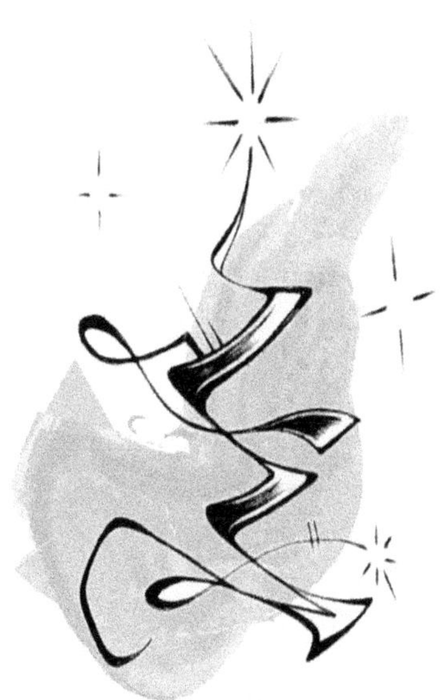

Abstrak Urban Consep2all Poetik

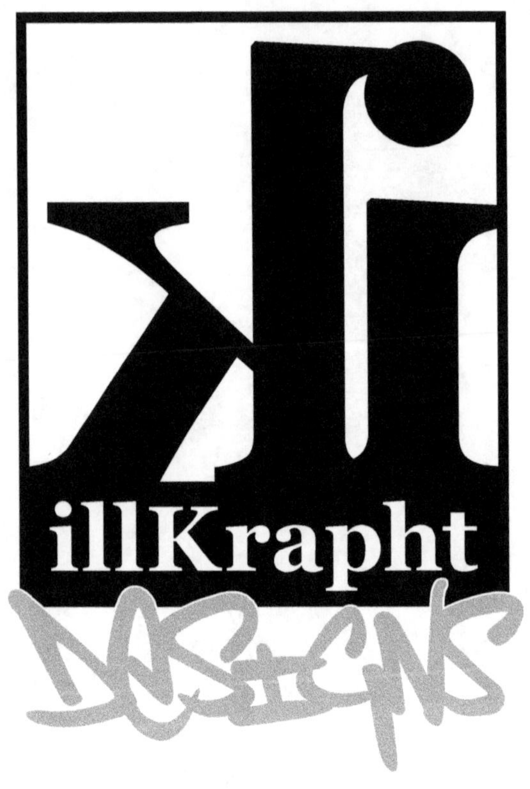

ART CREATION IS THE DOCUMENTATION OF THE SOUL'S VOICE

www.ingramcontent.com/pod-product-compliance
Lightning Source LLC
LaVergne TN
LVHW010942110826
845149LV00013B/2728

* 9 7 8 0 9 9 1 6 5 3 1 4 0 *